GODS & GODDESSES OF THE ANCIENT WORLD

Loki

BY VIRGINIA LOH-HAGAN

Gods and goddesses were the main characters of myths. Myths are traditional stories from ancient cultures. Storytellers answered questions about the world by creating exciting explanations. People thought myths were true. Myths explained the unexplainable. They helped people make sense of human behavior and nature. Today, we use science to explain the world. But people still love myths. Myths may not be literally true. But they have meaning. They tell us something about our history and culture.

45th Parallel Press

Published in the United States of America by Cherry Lake Publishing
Ann Arbor, Michigan
www.cherrylakepublishing.com

Content Adviser: Alexandra Krasowski, Worcester Art Museum, Harvard University (Extension School)
Reading Adviser: Marla Conn MS, Ed., Literacy specialist, Read-Ability, Inc.
Book Design: Jen Wahi

Photo Credits: Viktor Rydberg/Public Domain/Wikimedia Commons, 5; Arthur Rackham/Public Domain/Wikimedia Commons, 6, 24; © andreiuc88/Shutterstock.com, 8; Lorenz Frolich/Public Domain/Wikimedia Commons, 11; © Dundanim/Shutterstock.com, 13; W.G. Collingwood/Public Domain/Wikimedia Commons, 15; © Anetlanda/Shutterstock.com, 17; © umnola/Shutterstock.com, 19; © Hein Nouwens/Shutterstock.com, 23; © Svjetlana Peric/Shutterstock.com, 27; Louis Moe/Public Domain/Fra Dansk Skolemuseum, 29; © Howard David Johnson, 2018, Cover, 1, 21; Various art elements throughout, Shutterstock.com

45th Parallel Press is an imprint of Cherry Lake **Publishing.**

Library of Congress Cataloging-in-Publication Data

Names: Loh-Hagan, Virginia, author.
Title: Loki / by Virginia Loh-Hagan.
Description: Ann Arbor : Cherry Lake Publishing, 2018. | Series: Gods and goddesses of the ancient world | Includes bibliographical references and index.
Identifiers: LCCN 2018003336 | ISBN 9781534129467 (hardcover) | ISBN 9781534131163 (pdf) | ISBN 9781534132665 (pbk.) | ISBN 9781534134362 (hosted ebook)
Subjects: LCSH: Loki (Norse deity)—Juvenile literature.
Classification: LCC BL870.L6 L64 2018 | DDC 293/.2113—dc23
LC record available at https://lccn.loc.gov/2018003336

Printed in the United States of America
Corporate Graphics

ABOUT THE AUTHOR:

Dr. Virginia Loh-Hagan is an author, university professor, former classroom teacher, and curriculum designer. She loves teasing people. But she's too lazy to plan tricks. She lives in San Diego with her very tall husband and very naughty dogs. To learn more about her, visit www.virginialoh.com.

TABLE OF CONTENTS

CHAPTER 1

LOKI THE GIANT TRICKSTER

Who is Loki? What does he look like? Who are his family members?

Loki was a trickster god. He liked to fool people. He lied. He cheated. He stole. He liked to cause **mayhem**. Mayhem is disorder. Loki was the god of **mischief**. Mischief is trouble. Loki was also the god of fire. He was the god of magic.

Loki was a giant. His parents were both giants. His brothers were giants. Most giants and gods hated each other. They fought all the time. But Loki spent time with both the giants and gods. He kept Odin and Thor company. Odin and Thor were **Norse** gods. Norse means from the Norway area. Odin was the father of the gods. Thor was the god of thunder.

Some stories say Loki was Odin's foster brother.

Loki was the most mysterious god.

Loki lived in **Asgard**. Asgard was the universe's center. It was heaven. It was where the Aesir gods lived. There were two tribes of Norse gods and goddesses. They were the Aesir and the Vanir.

Loki was handsome. He had a big nose. He liked dancing. He often **sneered**. Sneers are mocking smiles. They're curls of the lips. Loki had magical powers. He could

Family Tree

Grandparent: Ymir (first giant)

Parents: Farbauti (frost giant; his name means "striker") and Laufey (frost giantess; her name means "leaves")

Brothers: Helblindi (frost giant; his name means "blinder") and Byleistr (frost giant; his name means "lightning")

Spouses: Angrboda (giantess; her name means "distress-bringer"), Sigyn (goddess; her name means "friend of victory"), and Svadilfari (male horse; his name means "traveler")

Children: Hel (goddess of death), Jormungand (world serpent), Fenrir (wolf), Sleipnir (Odin's eight-legged horse), and Narfi (his name means "corpse")

shapeshift. This means he could change into anything. He could take any living being's form. He'd been a fish. He'd been a horse. He'd been a fly. He could also change **gender**. Gender means being male or female. Loki also changed into an old woman.

Loki married Sigyn. Sigyn was a goddess. Her name means "friend of victory." Loki and Sigyn had a son. His name was Narfi. This means "**corpse**." Corpses are dead bodies.

Loki also married Angrboda. Angrboda was a **giantess**. Giantess means female giant. Loki and Angrboda had three scary children. Their names were Hel, Fenrir, and Jormungand. Hel was the goddess of death. Fenrir was a wolf. Jormungand was a snake.

Loki turned into a female horse. He gave birth to Sleipnir. Sleipnir was a horse. It had eight legs. Odin rode Sleipnir.

Loki liked playing tricks.

CHAPTER 2

LOKI THE HERO

How did Loki help the gods? Who is Freya? Who is Skadi? Who is Idun?

Loki could be helpful. He helped Freya. Freya was the goddess of beauty and war. Giants attacked Asgard. The gods needed walls to keep the giants away. A builder was hired. He wanted to marry Freya. The gods promised Freya to him. But the builder had to finish in a year and a day. The gods didn't think he could do it. But the builder had a magical horse. The horse did twice as much work. The builder was going to win. The gods asked Loki for help. Loki tricked the builder. He changed into a female horse.

He lured the builder's horse away. The wall couldn't be built. Freya was saved.

Loki would get the gods into trouble. Then he would save them. This made him look like a hero. Loki caused Skadi's father's death. Skadi was a giantess. She attacked Asgard. She wanted to get even. She wanted three things. First, she wanted a husband. Second, she wanted her father's eyes to become stars. Third, she wanted the gods to make her laugh.

Loki's tricks often hurt others.

All in the Family

Ice and fire mixed. A drop of water fell. This made Ymir. Ymir was the first being. He was a giant. He fell asleep. He sweated. His arm sweat formed a male and a female giant. His leg sweat formed a giant with six heads. He made more frost giants. He drank from a magical cow. This was how he stayed alive. The cow ate salt from rocks. It licked the rocks into the shape of a man. This became Buri. Buri was grandfather to Odin. Odin was a Norse god. He and his brothers killed Ymir. They used his flesh to make the earth. They used his skull to make the sky. They used his brain to make clouds. They used his bones to make mountains. They used his teeth to make rocks. They used his hair to make trees. They used his blood to make seas. Ymir's blood drowned all but one frost giant.

Loki thought he was funny.

The gods tried to make her laugh. They couldn't. But Loki did. He saved the day. Loki got a goat. He played tug-of-war with the goat. He cried in pain. He fell in Skadi's lap. This made Skadi laugh. The gods were saved.

In another story, Loki hurt and helped Idun. A giant wanted to kill Loki. Loki had to bring him Idun. He needed to do this to save his life. Idun was the goddess of spring. She was in charge of the golden apples. These made the gods **immortal**. Immortal means to live forever. The gods ate the apples to stay young. Loki led Idun into the woods. The giant turned into an eagle. He kidnapped Idun. This made the gods mad. Loki promised to fix his mistake. He turned into a falcon. He turned Idun into a nut. He took her back to Asgard.

Loki challenged the gods. He pushed them to change.

CHAPTER 3

EVIL LOKI

Who is Baldur? What is Loki's most evil trick?

Sometimes, Loki was a hero. But mostly, he was a **sidekick**. Sidekicks are like partners. Loki played tricks. He annoyed the gods. He shamed them. The gods were tired of his tricks. They grew to dislike him. This made Loki mad. He became evil. His worst trick was killing Baldur. Baldur was the god of light. He was the son of Odin and Frigg. Frigg was the goddess of marriage.

Baldur had dreams of dying. He told his parents. Frigg was worried. She went around the world. She begged people not to hurt Baldur. But Frigg didn't think mistletoe was a problem. She thought it wasn't important. She thought it was too little to do harm.

She went back to the gods' meeting hall. She told Baldur he was safe. She hosted a party. The gods wanted to test Baldur's protection. They threw things at Baldur. Things bounced off him. Baldur didn't get hurt.

Loki went on many adventures with the gods.

Real World Connection

James Linton is British. He's a web designer. He's also an email prankster. He tricked many people. He made fake email accounts. He pretended to be famous people. Then he emailed other famous people. He talked to them. He got them to tell him things. He posted their chats online. He used over 150 fake email accounts. He pranked people in the White House. He pranked heads of banks. He pranked movie stars. But then he made a mistake. He made a fund-raising account. He asked people for money to pay for his pranks. He gave away too much personal information. People found out who he was. So, he quit. His secret name was sinon_reborn. He took this name from a Greek story. Sinon was a Greek warrior. He convinced the people of Troy to let in the Trojan horse. Many enemy warriors hid in the wooden horse.

The gods lived in grand houses called halls.

This made Loki mad. He didn't like when others were happy. He insulted the gods. He tricked Frigg. Frigg told him about mistletoe. Loki used that information. He made a mistletoe dart. He told Hod to aim the dart at Baldur. Hod was Baldur's twin brother. He was blind.

Loki guided Hod's hand. Hod threw the dart at Baldur. The dart killed Baldur.

Baldur's light was gone. This created winter. The gods were mad at Loki. Loki ran away. The gods tried to get Baldur from the **underworld**. The underworld was where dead souls lived. It was also called hell. It was ruled by Hel. Hel played a trick. She said she'd release Baldur if all living things cried for him.

The gods begged everyone to cry for Baldur. But Loki stepped in. He disguised himself as Thok. Thok was a giantess. She refused to cry. So, Baldur stayed in hell.

The gods were scared of Loki's children.

CHAPTER 4

PUNISHED!

How does Loki escape? How does he get caught? How is he punished?

Loki ran away from Asgard. He hid on a mountaintop. He built a house with four doors. This was so he could keep watch from all sides. During the day, he turned into a fish. He hid under a waterfall. At night, he made a net. He used it to catch fish. No one thought of this before.

Odin found Loki. The gods went after him. They knew Loki was a fish. They made a net with Loki's things.

They tried to catch him. They missed. Loki tried to jump into the sea. Thor caught him in the air. Loki moved around. Thor held him tightly. He held his fish tail. Loki turned back into a giant. The gods took him to a cave.

Stories say that salmon have slender tails because of Thor's grip.

Sigyn placed the bowl over Loki.

Loki was punished for Baldur's death. They let a wolf kill Loki's son. The gods used Narfi's guts to make a chain. They tied Loki down with the chain. They tied him to three rocks. This trapped him inside the cave. They placed a snake above him. The snake dripped poison down onto his head. But Sigyn stayed with Loki. She had a bowl.

She held it above Loki. She caught the poison in her bowl. The bowl would fill up. Drops fell on Loki. He was in pain. It caused earthquakes.

Cross-Cultural Connection

Anansi was in many African stories. He was a trickster. He was a spirit. He changed shapes. He often took the form of a spider. But he's also been a rabbit, human, and fox. His father was the sky god. Anansi followed his father's orders. He was wise. He had all the world's wisdom. He put it in a pot. He kept it for himself. He didn't trust humans with the power. But wisdom kept leaking out. He realized it was better to share the wisdom. He taught lessons by playing tricks. He led people to the truth. He helped humans. He created the sun. He created the moon. He created the stars. He created the planets. He brought rain to stop fires. He gave writing to mankind. He gave them farming and hunting. But he was also selfish. His goal was to make himself happy. He fooled others to get what he wanted.

CHAPTER 5

THE LAST TRICK

What is Ragnarok? How do Loki and his children fight in the war? How does Loki die?

Baldur's death broke the peace among gods and giants. Loki's trick started **Ragnarok**. This was the final battle. It was the end of the world. It was known as the "doom of the gods."

Loki broke loose from his chain. He became the enemy of the gods. He fought against them. He led an army of giants. He released his children. The gods had trapped Hel in the underworld. They had thrown Jormungand into the sea. They had chained Fenrir to a big rock.

Loki's children helped him. Hel gave Loki an army of dead soldiers. Jormungand caused the seas to flood. His poison killed Thor. Fenrir ran around the world. His lower jaw was on the ground. His upper jaw was in the sky. He ate everything in his way. He ate the sun. He killed Odin.

Baldur's winter lasted 3 years.

Loki fought Heimdall. Heimdall was a god. He guarded the rainbow bridge. It was a bridge that connected to the

Explained By Science

Some people have gigantism. This is a rare disorder. It's caused by increased levels of growth hormones. Hormones are natural chemicals in the body. Gigantism happens around age 13. There are strange tumors on the pituitary gland. This gland is at the base of the brain. It makes growth hormones. Gigantism makes people grow very tall. People also grow wider. They're much larger than other people. They have big hands. They have big feet. They have thick toes. They have thick fingers. Their teeth spread out. Their jaw juts out. They have big foreheads. They have flat noses. They have large heads. They have large lips. They have large tongues. Their organs get big. They have patches of brown skin. They have headaches. They can't see well. They feel sick. They sweat a lot. They have sleeping problems. They don't live as long as others.

Baldur came back to life after Ragnarok.

human world. Loki and Heimdall killed each other. While they fought, Loki's army set the world on fire. The fire killed humans. It killed giants. It killed gods. The earth sank into the sea. Then it rose again. The world started over.

Don't anger the gods. Loki had great powers. And he knew how to use them.

DID YOU KNOW?

- Loki's name is connected to the words for nets and knots. He was a maker of nets. Nets are made of knots and loops. They're like webs. Loki trapped gods in his tricks.
- Spiders are sometimes called loki.
- Loki had the gift of flyting. Flyting is a contest. It's an exchange of insults. People talk in poems.
- Sif was known for her beautiful golden hair. Loki took some of Sif's hair. He did this as a joke. Sif was Thor's wife. Thor got mad. Loki made up for his trick. He gave her a golden wig. It was made by dwarfs.
- Loki was also known as the "prince of lies."
- Loki was one of the top three Norse gods. The other gods are Thor and Odin. These three gods appear in the most Norse stories.
- Loki made a bet with a dwarf. The dwarf was named Brok. Loki lost. So, Brok sewed Loki's mouth shut.
- Loki's face was on an old stone. The stone is over 1,000 years old. It was found in Denmark. It was found in 1950.
- Loki was in Marvel's *Thor* movies. He's shown as a villain. Villains are bad guys.
- Loki was compared to Prometheus. Prometheus was a Greek giant. He tricked Zeus. Zeus was the king of the gods. Zeus got mad at Prometheus. He chained him to a rock. An eagle ate his liver during the day. The liver grew back at night.

CONSIDER THIS!

TAKE A POSITION! Loki could help others. He could also cause harm. Was Loki good or bad? Was he a hero or a villain? Why do you think so? Argue your point with reasons and evidence.

SAY WHAT? Read the 45th Parallel Press about Thor. Thor and Loki are often pitted against each other. Compare them. Explain how they're the same. Explain how they're different.

THINK ABOUT IT! Think about a time you've been tricked. What happened? Who tricked you? Why were you tricked? How were you tricked? How did the trick make you feel?

LEARN MORE

Crossley-Holland, Kevin, and Jeffrey Alan Love (illust.). *Norse Myths: Tales of Odin, Thor and Loki.* Somerville, MA: Candlewick Studio, 2017.

Napoli, Donna Jo, and Christina Balit (illust.). *Treasury of Norse Mythology: Stories of Intrigue, Trickery, Love, and Revenge.* Washington, DC: National Geographic, 2015.

Worley, Rob M., and Brandon McKinney (illust.). *Loki.* New York: Looking Glass Library, 2010.

GLOSSARY

Asgard (AHS-gahrd) center of the universe where the Aesir gods lived

corpse (KORPS) dead body

gender (JEN-dur) being male or female

giantess (JYE-uhn-tis) female giant

immortal (ih-MOR-tuhl) living forever

mayhem (MAY-hem) chaos, disorder

mischief (MIS-chif) trouble, tricks, pranks

Norse (NORS) coming from the Norway area

Ragnarok (RAHG-nuh-rok) the final battle of the gods' world, marking the end of their world

shapeshift (SHAYP-shift) power to change shapes and take on different forms

sidekick (SIDE-kik) a partner who takes part in adventures

sneered (SNEERD) to smile mockingly

underworld (UHN-dur-wurld) the place where the souls of dead people go after they die

INDEX